Refusing To Quit

Refusing To Quit

*True Stories of Women over Sixty
Who Refused to Quit*

Joyce Knudsen, Ph.D.

The ImageMaker Inc. ® "Presents"

Refusing to Quit
Copyright © 2016 by Joyce Knudsen., Ph.D.
www.drjoyceknudsen.com

Published in the United States
ISBN 13: 978-151958150
ISBN 10: 151958156
Library of Congress Knudsen, Dr. Joyce – Author
152 pages

1. for the aging 2. Mental health 3. Happiness 4. Self-help 5.mid-life 6. Retirement 7. Inspiration 8. True stories 9. Changing times 10. Stages of aging 11. Mothers 12. Feel-good 13. Older women 14. Emotions 15. Seniors

FIRST EDITON
Cover Design © 2016 Brent Meske (facebook.com/bmeske)

This is a work of non-fiction. All rights remain reserved. Without limiting the rights under copyright reserved above, no part of this publication may be reproduced, stored in or introduced into a retrieval system, or transmitted, in any form, or by any means (electronic, mechanical, photocopying, recording or otherwise) without the prior written permission of both the copyright owner and Dr. Joyce Knudsen.

FOREWORD

In this wonderful book, Dr. Knudsen helps dismantle the prevalent stereotypes of older women and, thereby, helps younger women look forward to these years with an embrace that they ordinarily would not have had.

Our culture is replete with stifling archetypes about what it means to be of a certain gender. Women especially face rigid dictates of how to behave, look, and act. Couple this with being older and, suddenly, the woman over 60 is slammed with an inordinately high degree of prejudice. Antiquated belief systems make her vulnerable to a lowered self-esteem and sense of self.

It is now time to defy culture's way of narrowly defining our essence, be it man or woman, young or old. Our children and grandchildren deserve to live in a world where they can rest assured that who it is they are—at their deepest core—is valued far more greatly than what they do, how much money they make, or what they do for a living. When each being is valued for her inner gifts, which are replete in us all, we will then enter an age where tolerance for diversity of age, race, and ethnicity is valued above all.

This book makes an insightful contribution toward this new possibility. Dr. Knudsen's life is a testimony to how, if we believe in our inner essence, we can defy all odds. She is truly an example of how women at any age can overcome any obstacle and rise to their greatest potential.

Namaste,
Dr. Shefali Tsabary
Author of NYT Bestseller, *The Conscious Parent*
www.drshefali.com

TABLE OF CONTENTS

Foreword	viii
Dedication	xii
Acknowledgments	xiii
Special Acknowledgments	xv
Introduction	xvi
Changing Times	1
Self Esteem and Aging	4
Stages of the Aging Process	8

Remarkable Older Women

Dr. Connie Mariano	
Refuse to Accept Stereotypes	12
Sue Doherty	
Toward Thriving	16
Soraya Raju	
Passion Keeps Me Going	22
Ruthie Steele	
Detours on My Road to Fame and Fortune	28
Frieda Rapoport Caplan	
Never See Obstacles	32
Pam Friendlander	
My Positive Reflection	37
Ann Barros	
Beloved Bali Yoga	42
Cecily (CJ) Vermote	
Enjoying the Ride	47
Dr. Thynn Thynn	
Mindfulness and Bliss	52
Evelyn Lois Coy	
The Joy of Living	57
Linda Todd	
Unwilling to Settle	61
Rosemary Christie	
Determination	66
Carol Graham	
Quitting Was Never an Option	70
Colette Srebro Hughes	
Give Up the Bitter Cup	75

Jude L. Gorgopa
    An Awfully Big Adventure   80
LaVonne Phillips Mahugh
    Going On When Others...Quit   85
Sharon Boone
    Can't Stop–Won't Stop   90
Colette Michelle
    Be Empowered   95
Merle R. Saferstein
    Forever the Teacher   100
Mary McCormick
    On the Way to 105   105
Dr. Joyce M. Knudsen
    My Story   109

The Virtues of Aging   114
Summary and Conclusion   118
Epilogue   122
References   126

DEDICATION

This book is dedicated to my daughter, Kristen and beautiful granddaughter, Sydney. I hope one day, you too will be strong women over 60. I know in my heart that you will be.

ACKNOWLEDGMENTS

First and foremost, I would like to thank Dr. Shefali Tsabary, author of New York Times bestseller, *The Conscious Parent*, for writing a beautiful foreword for this book. To contact Dr. Shefali, go to: www.drshefali.com

I am grateful to Brent Meske for going the extra mile for me. Who says social site friends are not friends? I consider Brent a good friend because he believes in me and in my work. He is always right there to help me produce the finest books with the most valued format, and puts his *extra touch* into each and every book I send to him. You will never know how much this means to me. Thank you, Brent. You are the best. To reach Brent, email: meskebrent@gmail.com

It is my pleasure to acknowledge all the lovely ladies who took the time to write their stories in this book. They are not afraid to let people know how old they are, and they are proud of being the women they were meant to be.

Dr. Connie Mariano, Sue Doherty, Soraya Raju, Ruthie Steele, Frieda Rapoport Caplan, Pam Friedlander, Ann Barros, Cecily (CJ) Vemote, Dr. Thynn Thynn, Evelyn Lois Coy, Linda Todd, Carol Graham, Colette Hughes, Jude Gorgopa, LaVonne Mahugh, Sharon Boone, Colette Michelle, Merle R. Saferstein, and Mary McCormick.

And to my readers, *thank you*. You inspire me to keep on keeping on. I hope you enjoy this book as much as I enjoyed writing it.

SPECIAL ACKNOWLEDGMENT

Special thanks go to Sue Doherty, who has greatly contributed to this book. She has been my mentor and friend and wrote a wonderful epilogue for the book. Thank you, Sue. You made writing this book more enjoyable for me. To reach Sue, email: storiesmatter@yahoo.com

INTRODUCTION

We see how many women of celebrity status recognized by the media for their work. But what about all the great women who are being "*thrown under the bus*" who are great contributors to our world? Where is the recognition for what they worked so hard to accomplish? Are women over 60 the "**Forgotten Generation?**"

I felt a need to write Refusing to Quit: True Stories of Women over Sixty Who Refused to Quit for the many women who do just that: refuse to quit—no matter what their circumstances were, where they came from and how they were brought up.

There seems to be prejudice against aging. So often when we see someone over the age of 50 on television or in magazines, typically they are either marginalized or portrayed as feeble or non-productive.

Nothing could be further from the truth!

What about 60, 70 or 80? Age is not just a number. It is our attitude toward that number and the way we make the decision not to quit.

I am one in this demographic. I turned 71 this past August, during the printing of this book. I plan to live a productive, long and fulfilling life.

We are adapting to the changes that stand before us, learning technology, running businesses and contributing to society; we are the majority of people who volunteer in organizations.

Yes, as we all look back in time, it seems like the years have gone by too quickly. Wasn't it just yesterday we were driving our children to school and baking cookies with them? Or, if you chose to work outside of the home, it seems such a short time ago that you started your career, and now you discover it's been 20 years! Where did the time go? How did we adapt?

This important topic of forgetting an entire segment of society is rarely written or spoken about throughout the media. The time is now for these women who are not celebrities or public figures to be recognized. I consider it *"my job"* to recognize them.

I've been adapting since an early age, due to a fever as a baby, which damaged my eyesight and gave me limited vision. I knew that my sight would deteriorate as part of the natural aging process, but I never thought that I would be diagnosed with an eye condition that only 1-2% of the population has, and which professionals do not fully understand. This limitation did not stop me from forging ahead!

In my case, I did not allow my "limited vision" to stop me from anything I wanted to do. Instead of choosing to look at my situation in a negative way, I chose to set an example for others and make this lemon into lemonade. All one has to do is go to my website to see what I have accomplished. I have reached self-actualization in my personal life being happily married for 47 years (at the time of this printing), and also in professional life through owning my own business for over 30 years. And, YES, so can anyone else. My feeling was that if I could not have vision for myself, I would have vision for others and for the world.

I applaud these great women who have chosen not to retire and quit just because they were aging. These women see no reason to retire, as their *"vocation" is their "vacation."* These women love to work! They relish being productive, have amazing goals and pursue them.

The time is **NOW** for women over 60 to be recognized for their worthwhile contribution to society.

~Dr. Joyce

1

Changing Times

Times have changed. In years past, "the rule of thumb" used to be a one-family income with dad going to work and mom taking care of the children. Those days are gone.

We have moved into two family incomes, and many times parents are forced to send the children to daycare while they go to work. More than ever before, women are in the workforce. Generations think differently about how they want to spend their time. While many mothers years ago cherished their time at home, the women of today like or need their independence working outside the home.

Have the generational changes affected the way we look at retirement? When younger people interpret the word retirement, what do they think? Retirement has different meanings to those under the age of 60; however, once becoming women 60 or over, they have to think about what they are going to do as an "older person." Will they enter the workforce for the first time? Will they stop working at one career and enter another? Will they even have a choice? How long can they expect to live? Are they married, single or divorced? There are many considerations that surface when deciding how to live out the rest of your life.

"By 2030, a 65-year-old American female can expect to live another 19.2 years on average (16.3 years on average for males). By the year, 2018, the participation of seniors 65 and older in the labor force is projected to grow nearly ten times faster than the total labor force. By 2030, the number of Americans over 65 will more than double," ~ Elizabeth F. Fideler, author, 2012.

When we used to think about aging, many people thought that was a time for retirement and felt they could do some things they had only considered before. Now, either a woman works out of necessity, or she does not want to leave a career she loves. Since the baby boomer generation is now the largest generation of women, there are more women over 60 in the workplace. Here are some reasons women are working during their later years:

- The recession

Refusing to Quit

- Collapse of investments
- Home value reinvention
- Satisfaction from contributions
- Social relationships
- Flexible careers
- Helping others
- Cost of living
- Dependence on Social Security
- Unhealthy spouse

Researchers asked people age 50 and older the reasons for continuing to work in their retirement years. According to USA Today, there are ten reasons why people continue to work:

- I want to keep earning money to retire more comfortably (53%).
- I would be bored not working (31%).
- I keep working because income from other sources is not enough (18%).
- I want to feel productive, useful, and helpful (18%).
- I have a job that is fun, enjoyable (15%).
- I want to interact with people (13%).
- I want to stay physically/mentally active (12%).
- I need health insurance (6%).
- I am pursuing my dream: I have a job doing what I want to (6%).
- I want to learn new things (2%).

Self-esteem and Aging

Beauty is a reflection of how the world views us, but true beauty is something that comes from within. It is how, deep down, we feel about ourselves.

Every day, it seems, there are new articles and reports published about how women deal with getting older. Occasionally, articles and comments are critical of women who try to look attractive as they age. Criticism can change one's personality. It's up to us to feel good about ourselves. It's up to us to design our life and desires at this time. It's up to us to refine our definition of retirement.

"What we think, feel and imagine, we become."

"Confront the dark parts of yourself at any age and work to banish them with illumination and forgiveness. Your willingness to wrestle with

your demons will cause your angels to sing." ~ Unknown

"Life is 10 percent what you experience and 90 percent how you respond to it." ~ Dorothy M. Neddermeyer

"Don't you dare, for one more second, surround yourself with people who are not aware of the greatness that you are." ~ Jo Blackwell-Preston

"Life is not easy for any of us. But, what of that? We must have perseverance and above all confidence in ourselves at any age. We must believe that we have gifts for something, and that this thing, at whatever cost, must be attained." ~ Marie Curie

Having positive self-esteem is relevant for older people. Self-esteem links to the following six variables:

- The ability to be adaptive when faced with life changes
- Being happy with life
- Quality of adaptation
- Well-being
- Life satisfaction
- Health

Thus, it is critical that we look past chronological age (the number of years a person has lived) to biological age. It's more important to consider the person's quality of social integration and adaptive capacities to cope with life events, including physical and cognitive decline.

To be the older woman who can expand her mind and move on with her life, she needs to embrace her good feelings about herself. Aging doesn't have to result in the lowering of esteem, even if and when she begins to decline in areas of mental activity.

According to research studies, a woman's level of self-esteem, at this time in her life, will vary. Being involved with groups and by maintaining power through continued self-actualization, a woman can increase self-esteem. Self-actualization has been defined as the motive to realize one's full potential, the need to be good, to be fully alive and to find meaning in life. Also by expressing one's creativity, quest for spiritual enlightenment, pursuit of knowledge, and the desire to give to society. She must continue to move on and not give up on her goals and dreams.

"Ultimately, it is not age that matters—it is how we adapt to the changing nature of the workplace, manage to still love what we do and

contribute. This is likely true throughout our career lives." ~ Dr. Marla Gottschalk

Stages of the Aging Process

Some people get to the age of 60 before they say to themselves, "I've suddenly realized I'm getting old," while others may never think they are old. They live their entire lives enjoying the wisdom they have acquired through years of working at a profession and/or being there for their children and grandchildren. They are happier now than ever!

Aging is an individual thing. However, there are stages to the aging process that need to be considered. Not all people go through stages, which don't necessarily occur in any order or at any specific age.

<u>Stage One</u>: Physical Changes.

Things are happening to our bodies. Our skin is sagging, and as you look around, you are well aware you are no longer young.

Stage Two: Comparison.

We look at pictures and see how we once appeared and realize we are not that person anymore. You may see the "old me" compared to how you look, feel and act today. Research indicates that if we like the "me" we are as an older person, we are happy people. If we don't like the "me" we've become, we feel regret.

One way of beginning to compare may occur when our parents become older or pass away. We know we will always be children in our parents' hearts and minds but, at some point, we come to realize we have become adults and our parents are aging. When this happens, no matter what age you are, at this time, you will realize that you were very young in comparison to your parents and realize why they always referred to you as children.

When our role switches to being the caretaker, the tables are turned. Suddenly, our parents are the children, and we are the adults. Although this time of our life can be unsettling, it is something we need to do. No longer is your time your own. Your parents need you.

Stage Three:

Learning to Adapt.

This stage means we accept ourselves as older people. We send away our past and think about what we will be like in the present and future. Emotions have been released, and we can now accept our loss. At this time, we look forward to what we have. We accept the "me" we are now. This new "me" is moving on and will adjust with time.

<u>Stage Four</u>: Being Appreciative.

You have adapted to the older age, and in this stage you are ready to come to terms with full acceptance of your age.

Once going through these stages of aging, you can find new avenues for growth. Perhaps you have always wanted to take the time to exercise. Maybe you always imagined doing something for your community, but you never had the time to take the time or make a difference when you were younger.

Through the many profiles that follow, all one has to do is read to see that women in their 60s and older are refusing to quit.

Refusing to Quit

Disclaimer- The stories written have only been changed for typographic errors, because I felt it important not to change the "feel" of their heartfelt words.

What follows are twenty stories of women who are sixty and over but who refuse to quit!

Refuse to Accept Stereotypes

Written by Dr. Connie Mariano

Refusing to Accept Stereotypes

Dr. Connie Mariano/ Scottsdale, Arizona: Age 60

I celebrated my sixtieth birthday in January 2015 in typical fashion for my atypical life. Sporting a rhinestone tiara and size two cocktail dress, I enjoyed the toasts by close friends, two wonderful sons, and my handsome 59-year-old husband of five years.

Throughout my life, I've defied stereotypes and instead, defined my journey. I grew up constantly reminded that I didn't fit the stereotype for an American girl. My parents were born in the Philippines. My father was a U. S. Navy serviceman, and we moved every two years. Growing up in the 1960s in America as a Navy "brat," I struggled to fit in. Eventually, I surrendered and embraced the fact that I did not fit anyone's stereotype. That realization freed me to become the White House doctor to three sitting American presidents. Also, I achieved the rank of Rear Admiral in the U. S. Navy, becoming the first American of Filipino descent to earn this honor.

After 24 years in the Navy, the last nine at the White House, I moved to Scottsdale, Arizona to work at the Mayo Clinic. Joining the non-profit medical group was to be my "retirement" job at the age of 46. But I was not ready, nor tired, to retire. I saw patients at the Mayo Clinic until it was time for a new chapter in my life: private practice.

On my fiftieth birthday, I opened my concierge medical practice in Scottsdale. The practice grew to over 300 patients consisting of CEOs and their families. While my practice flourished, my 29-year marriage expired. At 53, I divorced my husband. I left him for "another woman": me.

The seven years leading to my 60th birthday defined the new "me." In addition to growing my practice, I signed with St. Martin's Press to publish my memoir of my White House years. In the midst of seeing patients, writing my book, and spending time with my college-aged sons, I fell in love.

At 55, I married a former patient of mine who was a CEO of an auto-parts company. Although it was my second marriage, I felt as though I were a young bride. My husband and I are proof that it's never too late to live happily ever after.

Refusing to Accept Stereotypes

My 60th birthday was the first without my mother. She passed away the month before. Eight months after my mother died, my first grandchild was born. As I held my granddaughter for the first time, I reflected upon my life and thought how different my granddaughter's life will be. She was welcomed into a family that loved her from the start. Her future had endless possibilities.

A wise woman once said, "To have a good life you need three things: 1) Someone to love, 2) Something to do, and 3) Something to look forward to."

At 60, I'm married to the love of my life. When it comes to "things to do" my list is long: private practice, writing more books, and speaking engagements.

There are many things I look forward to in the next 40 years. One is to watch my granddaughter grow up. I intend to be her mentor and biggest cheerleader. I plan to teach her that life is a gift and every day we should ask God, "What do you want me to do today to serve you?" I will teach her not to be afraid, to reject stereotypes, and most of all, to refuse to quit.

Toward Thriving

Written by Sue Doherty

Toward Thriving

Sue Doherty/Aptos, California: Age 63

It was on my thirteenth birthday I had to have spinal surgery to fuse 12 vertebrae. If nothing else, a year in a body cast enforced contemplation, patience, and a wider degree of resilience. It also initiated self-healing, as I visualized a straight, bionic spine made to endure anything. Once free of the plaster, movement became a source of salvation from pain. At times, I would walk four miles to high school and eight to college, just for the love of the stride.

My back could feel annoyingly numb, sharp, and constricted. That eased after I was befriended by the Nathan Pritikin family and converted to the father's revolutionary vegetarian diet. As if aligning with the natural forces of my body, I began to feel so much lighter, with better circulation and more energy. It was rejuvenating; the enticement to forgo the last year of college for an expedition became irresistible.

Sue Doherty

With my fiancé, I found myself working on the pipeline outdoors in the frigid Arctic as the only woman operating engineer. We homesteaded land and built a two-story log cabin from scratch in the Alaskan bush. Then we planned for and kayaked 1,100 miles in 44 days down the longest and most remote river in North America, crossing the Continental Divide and down the Porcupine and Yukon Rivers. These are peak experiences that kept me going for a long time. Sometimes experiences lock you into that vital space of belief in yourself. Self-efficacy develops–that lingering "can do" attitude that comes from believing in the wisdom of your choices and values, and admiration for your spirit and strength.

Exercise, healthy eating, and peak experiences may be cliché, but their outcomes are not. The embodied sense of well-being becomes an authority to which you willingly relinquish power. Spontaneous living and the rapture of authenticity became likewise compelling. I was examining my life at every turn. Reading eastern mysticism and practicing yoga and meditation became regular retreats. A more refined sense of self-knowledge began to emerge–I was becoming more alert, attentive, and aware. The quests continued.

After traveling to Europe, Morocco, and Central America, we settled in Boston for reasons

Toward Thriving

of higher education. Stepping into the city's enormous main library, I found the category for science and medicine and became engrossed in a book on acupuncture. Serendipitously, I picked up a local telephone book and discovered the proximity of The New England School of Acupuncture. I enrolled in this pioneering program and was among the first in the country to graduate with a master's in acupuncture. My career path was set.

After six years away from the Bay Area, we returned to northern California. But, at the time, unbeknownst to me, the state did not accept the school's accreditation. Discouraged, I lifted my spirits by teaching myself how to play the mandolin and by going back to college. I gained certification in holistic nutrition, began consulting, and also started freelance writing.

As a young mother, I ritually did yoga, tai chi, and dancing with my babies. I saw how we mutually thrived while playing in this way together. I began to wonder: why is it that when a baby is in our arms we instinctively rock it back and forth, especially to music, and why does the baby like it so much? It became an obsession of sorts, eventually compelling me to write a book on the subject: *Kinergetics: Dancing With Your Baby for Bonding and Better Health for Both of You.* It took several years of persistent writing, editing, and marketing to get finally published in 1994. It also led to a bachelor's and master's in anthropology, thanks to the mentoring of the renowned anthropologist, Ashley Montagu.

"Experiences over possessions" and "life-long learning" are mottos I have always held dear. So, when our family had the opportunity for a year sabbatical in Tamarindo, Costa Rica, we took it. I immersed myself in Spanish and doing cultural landscape fieldwork. During the immediate years afterward, adjusting back to full-time work schedules became uninviting; we soon opted to slow down to part-time work and traveling. My mind started stirring over possibilities of updating the book. Scientific evidence was mounting in several relevant disciplines, from infant development and the brain sciences to music and dance therapy. I decided to do some anthropological fieldwork by working with hard of hearing infants and toddlers.

I began the goal of rewriting *Dancing with Your Baby*. I circulated a couple dozen first draft manuscripts to infant development labs and otherwise pertinent professionals. After years of continuous updating and numerous attempts to get traction, the eBook was beautifully edited and published in the summer of 2014, and a print version in spring of 2015. I am extremely grateful to the people who have nurtured its release and others who have supported it.

These last several years living in Santa Cruz County and working with children and teens with special needs have been very gratifying. Gratitude is a powerful tool that gives us the grace to continue. I will never "give up" on trying to live an authentic and mindful life, and exploring and sharing how we may thrive through the life cycle. At age 63, I'm only getting started!

Passion Keeps Me Going

Written by Soraya Devi Raju

Passion Keeps Me Going

Soraya Devi Raju/ Sydney, Australia: Age 64

When my father died, the Hindu funeral rites required my mother to be dressed in her marriage sari and bridal jewelry. "From now on you are a widow, and you will dress in white," were the cruel words that ripped away her life as a devoted wife and mother.

Those words destroyed her and her zest for life. Aged just 53 years, she became completely dependent on me. From the end of her career until her death at the age of 73, I experienced, at close hand, her helplessness to be even the shadow of the woman she might have been. I chose a different journey. Quitting is not an option.

Born in Malaysia to Indian parents with foresight, I went to a convent school where the nuns and teachers taught us that anything is possible. In a country and culture not well known for enlightened views about women, those wonderful women made sure we knew that being a girl did not matter.

My parents gave me the best education money could buy– a combination of East and West. My first experience of Australia was as a young schoolgirl—more or less alone in a strange country. A university education followed, but coming from an Asian country and a different culture meant those years were tough. Speaking English was, however, a great asset, and I was determined to make the best use of the great opportunities that were available in Australia.

After graduating with a degree in economics and accounting, I returned to Malaysia for family reasons and work. It was almost as challenging going back to my country of birth as it had been to settle in Australia. I had to reacquaint myself with a different cultural and working environment than I had become accustomed to in Australia. Working in a male environment, I had to prove myself.

I returned to the corporate world and pursued a role in senior management. After a long, successful career I received a humbling acknowledgment from a financial services magazine that profiled me in an article titled "Creative Compliance." This play on my compliance role at my work and my creative style in my dressing planted a seed for my future that I was yet to realize fully.

Working in the highly competitive, male-oriented financial sector, I developed my creative side. Exposure to the arts and various cultures surrounding me in multicultural Australia helped me to develop an interest in my heritage, in particular, in the 1,000 saris inherited from my mother who was a great collector.

Passion Keeps Me Going

Focusing on the history of sari fashion over a 40-year period gave added strength to my membership of an enthusiastic textile society and generated invitations to make presentations on my sari collection.

Exploring the various ways (more than 120) of wearing saris in India led me to give a presentation titled 'India's gift to the West: a modern take on the traditional sari.' Toastmasters and the enjoyment of sharing my knowledge with like-minded people helped me to hone my skills as a speaker.

Meanwhile, a new direction was opening up new opportunities. Friends and colleagues admired my sartorial style and started asking me to help them with shopping and dressing. I found I enjoyed helping others with their image. Voted one of Malaysia's best-dressed executives in 1986 by Her World Magazine, I knew the importance of first impressions. What had started as a hobby led me to become an image consultant. Eventually, I left the corporate world to follow my passion. Obtaining the necessary qualifications was the first step towards beginning a new career in image presence.

During this time, I started questioning my role in this world and started thinking about my contribution to society. I decided it was time to give something back to the community. Some years ago, I began volunteering with 'Dress for Success,' a voluntary organization dedicated to the promotion of economic independence of disadvantaged women by providing professional attire. I have found it a totally fulfilling experience.

One of their programs helps women who are interned in the prison system. As a result of being involved with this program, I have learned not to make quick judgments of other people. Most of the inmates come from disadvantaged backgrounds and suffer from low self-esteem. Now in my 60s, once again, there are big changes with which to deal.

Instead, I started exploring what else I could do and did a course in teaching English as a second language. This experience has brought me in touch with a new group of people–migrants and refugees with specific needs that I feel are well suited to my skill set. Now it's time to review my business model and breathe new life into it. So I am rebranding my business to be called 'Mi Gr8 Success'–which provides professional help with image presence, social and business etiquette, and with learning our unique style of Australian English.

My goal is to draw on my experience in the corporate and volunteer sectors to assist others coming into our beautiful country to settle into the working and social environment. My focus is to help migrants quickly assimilate, so they can easily move into high-level managerial jobs in the corporate sector or even start a new business.

An artist who wanted to paint my portrait and submit it for the Portia Geach Memorial Award 2015 for Australian women artists approached me recently. In this world that worships youth and beauty, I feel privileged to have been chosen as a subject for this prestigious award.

I have plans to write a book on the story of my mother's saris, and perhaps other subjects about my passion for textiles and other interests. I have started collecting stories from the migrants about their difficulties and successes in adapting to a new country. While I can, I will continue enjoying the world and helping others to achieve their dreams in life.

I will never stop working and refuse to quit. There is just too much to be done to make our world a better place.

Detours on My Road to Fame and Fortune

Written by Ruthie Barnes Steele

Detours on My Road to Fame and Fortune

Ruthie Barnes Steele/ Nashville, TN: Age 82

My story begins with my love for music, which I learned from my gramma that played the piano and my dad who played the fiddle. I've been a country music fan since I was very little. I was only eight years old when I wrote my first song.

I was born Ruth Ann Barnes, the seventh child. My dad was a mechanic; he was considered a "shade tree mechanic," which meant that he did his work at home in his yard.

At age 14, I was able to babysit in the neighborhood and do chores for neighbors to earn a few dollars to buy an old beat-up second-hand guitar. My brother, who was in the Army, had formed a band. He told me if I learned my chords and memorized some country songs, he would hire me to be the female singer when he returned home.

At 15, I became professional. I also learned to sing harmony with him and other members of the band. I made the decision to leave school and go on the road with them.

Like most young girls of that era, I married young and started having babies. My first of six children was my son, David, who also became a lifelong music professional. In 2006 and 2007, both David and I were inducted into The American Old Time Country Music Hall Of Fame.

As time went by, I learned to play six instruments and had an agent for many years. In 1967, my agent took me to Nashville with a briefcase full of simply-recorded demos of about 20 of the songs I had written and recorded. In those days, I never used co-writers, and I always sung the songs with my own backup harmony. My agent was hoping to get me signed as a staff writer for Nashville's then famous, Cedarwood Publishing Company, and they signed me! They also fell in love with my voice and offered me a recording contract with their record label, Jed Records.

Somewhere along the way my agent, Mitch Karem, and I invented a comedy character for me, Nashville Nelly, and Nelly joined up with a 10-piece country band called Nashville Review. We traveled in a beautiful tour bus all over the USA to open shows for Opry Stars. Later, I opened my own Nashville music business booking agents, artist promotion, record producing and publishing company. I also produced several albums of my songs on an Indie label.

In 2013, Jeffrey Lucky Hodnett put out a new album of my songs called *Ruthie Steele Songwriters Tribute Album* on Lucky 7 Records. Fourteen of my songs were songs performed by several other artists, and four that I performed myself. I recently (2015) made another new album. Artists put 13 of my songs on their albums.

To this day I still sing, play and write music, as well as record and build videos and websites: I do this to entertain people who love music as I do. At the age of 82, my life is still filled with music. I hope my music has contributed to the enjoyment and pleasure of many young people coming into the music business.

In the summer of 2015, another album of Ruthie Steele songs became available on Amazon. The record is called *Love is Not Always a Rose*, recorded on the Forbidden Tears Label.

For Success –

Never See Obstacles

Written By Frieda Rapoport Caplan

Never See Obstacles

Frieda Rapoport Caplan/Long Beach, CA: Age 92

Frieda Caplan is a vibrant 92 years young at the time of this writing. Often compared to Julia Child, Frieda Caplan made specialty fruits and vegetables accessible to the average American in the same way Julia Child made French cooking accessible to everyday home cooks. Frieda revolutionized the male-dominated produce industry in the 1960s. We can thank Frieda and her company for introducing kiwifruit, habanero peppers, spaghetti squash, and a list of more than 200 items over the past 50-plus years. Today, Frieda still works daily at the wholesale produce company she founded in Southern California. – Hazel Kelly, Co-Producer, Fear No Fruit: The Frieda Caplan documentary.

A young lady, who was about 32, looked at me and said, "Frieda, how does it feel to be old?" I looked at her and said, "Well, I've never figured I was beyond 18. I still feel the same way."

I started Frieda's Specialty Produce on the Los Angeles Wholesale Produce Market in 1962, but I did not have a business plan. Associates tell me that success came because I never saw obstacles. Ninety years had passed since Americans had met their last new fruit, the banana, in 1870 in Philadelphia. So when I introduced kiwifruit in 1962, people told me I was crazy, but that didn't stop me.

I was never aware, at that time, of how unusual it was that I was a woman in business on the LA Market. I never had a problem with the men on the market. Once they got over the fact that I was a woman, and they learned they could make money with the items I was selling, I had no problems.

People have called me the "Queen of Kiwi," "The Lady of Shallots," and the "Mick Jagger of the Produce World." But my success in marketing specialty fruits and vegetables probably had a lot to do with good luck, an open mind, and my positive outlook.

In late October of 1961, a couple of woman writers from the Los Angeles Times were walking by the produce market. They were stunned to see a woman on the market selling. They interviewed me and ran the article on Nov. 10, 1961, in the LA

Never See Obstacles

Times Family section. It read in part: "A sturdy brunette, mother of two, sets her alarm clock for 2 a.m. every weekday to enter a fascinating world known to very few..."

A few months later, the owners of Southern Pacific Railway came to me and said, "Frieda, we want you to go into business for yourself." I said, "You're kidding, not me!" I knew nothing about money, and I had no experience running a business. They said, "We've been watching you this last five or six years, and we are convinced you would be very successful, and you're selling something that's quite unusual." So I took the leap and never looked back.

Not long after opening Produce Specialties Inc., (now known as Frieda's Inc.) farmers began bringing unusual items to me – things that nobody else on the market would pay any attention to. We listened to everyone nobody listened to. Whoever had an idea, we listened. We had an open door policy and we believed in the potential of these new items. So I would bring in a new fruit or vegetable, introduce it, sample it, and find a few innovative buyers who knew that they had produce managers who would display it and sample it in store. It was that simple.

But we realized that just having a good product that looked interesting with food value was not enough, and this is where we learned to become produce marketers first, and wholesalers and distributers second. My strength was marketing, and, to this day, that is my strength. Running a business is not my strength. All the credit I get for so many things that Frieda's has accomplished, a great many of them, really, are due to my daughters, Karen and Jackie, who now run the business. My granddaughter, Alex, is also an up-and-coming account manager for Frieda's Inc. Having my daughters and granddaughter involved in the business has been one of my greatest joys.

My late mother always said my greatest strength was due to my optimistic, positive view of things. With my mom in mind, the most important message I can leave with is to be politically active. In order to participate in government, and in the world, you have to be knowledgeable. You have to be aware, and you have to realize there's more than one side to a situation. You have to understand both sides and what motivates people. Vote. Speak up. Whether it is about gun control, fracking, the Dream Act, or GMOs, don't sit silently by. Be a part of the action, and help make the world a better place.

I may be 92, but I've still got a lot to do. I don't look at it as something that is a very special life. I just have been a very lucky person.

My Positive Reflection

Written by Pam Friedlander

Pam Friedlander

Pam Friedlander/Danbury Connecticut: Age 68

I have never refused to quit. I have always had a burning desire to accomplish my goals. Although I went through what I feel was the long way around, I did it.

Going to college was so important to me. I knew I struggled in school, but I didn't know that I was not college material. At the time I decided to make my dreams happen, I didn't think much of it. I just did it. I applied to a community college non-matriculated night school and worked hard to achieve my grades, and catch up on classes I didn't take in high school. To me, graduating with an Associate Degree was a fantastic accomplishment. I then went on to get my Bachelor of Arts degree.

My first job was working as a group worker with senior citizens. (The seniors I worked with then are my age now). I decided to organize a chorus. I knew all the songs of their generation,

My Positive Reflection

but I didn't know how to read music. I refused to give up since I loved music and because of the fun and joy it would give to everyone being a part of this group. I found a senior who was a wonderful pianist. I knew how to sing, and she kept me in time. Together we made an incredible team. I remember saying to the group, "You are flat." I just kept keeping on, didn't quit, and loved every minute of it. We traveled to perform in other senior centers. I remember how proud they were.

After years in real estate and raising my son, I decided to go back to what I so enjoyed when I was young. I searched and searched until I came upon a job opportunity at an adult day care center, which I got. And eventually the director and I opened the first adult day care center in my town.

That touch of work success was gratifying, but I had an ongoing personal struggle with my weight. At age fifty-six and 200 pounds, I hated the way I looked and felt frustrated, disgusted, and angry. My mother had recently died, and I was mourning her loss. I knew I had one more diet left in me, so I went back to a 12-step program. The food plan worked because I knew it was my last chance, and I met great friends who had the same food issues. I lost 65 pounds and have kept it off for the past 11 years.

Shopping for my "mother of the groom" gown, I

found what just might be the perfect dress. Looking back at my reflection in the mirror was a woman I didn't recognize. I felt like Julia Roberts in "Pretty Woman": beautiful, elegant and thin.

Nine years ago, I began a new career in Image Management. The choice of a business name was crucial; it needed to reflect my "authentic self." I want to help women feel confident and beautiful. Positive Reflections was born—for the purpose of making other women feel great in their personal and professional presence. At the age of 68, I still enjoy this new career.

The woman that always had difficulty with her weight and school is still a part of me. That obstacle helps me understand what another woman is going through and how she feels about herself. A 'Positive Reflection' of ourselves is what I truly believe is important for the women that I work with and for myself. I do not think I would have gotten this far if it weren't for all the women in my life. I will always be grateful to them for encouraging me to expand my business.

Even now when I'm in a dressing room with women and am focusing only on her, I suddenly catch a glimpse of myself and am still surprised and pleased at my reflection. Looking back, I realize that I am the type of person that just does not want to give up, ever.

Today I feel confident when I walk into a room

and speak to women. I am proud of my business that I worked so hard to create. I have persevered, especially creating a website and staying up to date with social media, as I'm not a part of the digital generation. I refuse to let my fear of technology stop me from staying current. I've learned to ask for help from friends or people I employ. That high school girl who worked so hard to get a BA refuses to quit.

Beloved Bali Yoga

Written By Ann Barros

Ann Barros/Santa Cruz, California: Age: 65

I was walking to the beach, as I do every day, when a neighbor called out to me, "You're in this book, Eat, Pray, Love." Indeed I was. Author, Elizabeth Gilbert, on page 221, tells a medicine man in Indonesia, "I don't think you remember me, Ketut. I was here two years ago with an American yoga teacher, a woman who lived in Bali for many years." He smiles, elated, "I know Ann Barros!"

All the buzz about the best-selling book brought me a deluge of emails daily and more participants on my program than I'd seen since the 90s. I was riding the wave of a fantastic upswing in my Bali Yoga business. Many women wanted to recreate the Elizabeth Gilbert experience, which put me in a moral dilemma. Although I relished their enthusiasm and desire to join my program, I could not guarantee the same life altering epiphany that Gilbert experienced.

On my fall 2009 trip to Bali Yoga retreat, Hollywood burst into Ubud, Bali to film the movie. At the request of Ketut's nephew, I went to visit old Ketut at his home. The producer was there and explained to me how they were taking artistic license to change the story. I felt a bit rejected by Hollywood, but ever more committed to my career attracting the discriminating traveler seeking personal expertise and guidance into the real Bali.

The island had recovered from the devastating terrorist bombing in 2002, and so had my retreat program. In the aftermath of the tragedy, thousands of visitors had canceled their trips to Bali, but I had to come! I had to meet and talk with my Balinese friends, to see their friendly faces, hear their reactions, cry, and pray with them. I trembled at the thought of not being able to continue coming again and again.

Bali has been my life since 1980 when I first set foot on the island directly after intensive yoga training with Shri B.K.S. Iyengar in India. I was 31. I had an around the world ticket with the time to spare, and so spontaneously booked a flight to Bali. The aim was to reflect, to practice yoga on this Hindu island, and to ingest the yoga experience before returning to the West to pursue a professional dance career. A month of rapturous warm tropical air, friendly invitations, and meditations on my career path changed my plans;

Beloved Bali Yoga

I would become an Iyengar-certified yoga instructor. I vowed to myself that I would figure out a way to return to this beloved island filled with magic for the rest of my life. I have now completed 67 successful Bali Yoga retreats over the course of 30 years!

In 1998, I spontaneously started a garden accessories business of bamboo wind chimes. I enjoyed the soothing sounds of the chimes that I brought back from Bali that hung outside in my garden. Soon my students asked to purchase them because they enjoyed the serenade while in yoga class, which was in my garage converted yoga studio at my other paradise home on the California coastline. Soon this passion grew to selling to garden nurseries in nearby upscale areas. I received an enthusiastic response and an order for 50 chimes, which I confidently said I could deliver. My little wind chime business was lots of fun and flowed for several years. When the economy slowed down, I was ready to let the wholesale business go.

The constant in my life has always been and remains yoga. I am fortunately genetically flexible, but it's always been so much more than the flexibility to me. I love helping people understand their bodies. I loved my anatomy training and enjoy teaching in a very precise, anatomical approach. It is rewarding for me to experience a small class of yoga students releasing tensions and stress-related kinks of pain in their bodies, and breaking through fear barriers in challenging yoga poses. As my teacher, B.K.S. Iyengar, said, "Yoga teaches us to cure what need not be endured and endure what cannot be cured."

Imagine a self-employed yoga instructor owning her beach home property free and clear. This accomplishment has been my goal of a lifetime. In May 2015, I paid off my home mortgage in full. I am so grateful to have accomplished this goal.

I will continue to teach yoga and visit beloved Bali often; commune with my garden, indulge in barefoot walks on the beach, dance salsa that brings me great joy, laugh a lot, and be with friends. In my sixties, I feel more alive and vibrant than ever before. I am a woman who refuses to quit.

Enjoying the Ride

Written by Cecily (CJ) Vermote

Cecily (CJ) Vermote

Cecily (CJ) Vermote/Lynnwood, Washington: Age 65

I was born in Renton, Washington. As soon as I could write, I wrote poems to express my heart. Words flowed on paper with the swiftness of my pen. As a senior in high school, we were all assigned a subject for our term paper. Mine was on homosexuality.

Back in the 60s, this was more than the sensitive subject it is now. I spent the allotted time reading anything and everything to understand the subject. When I was done, my teacher gave me an A+, but it didn't end there. She said my work had the capability to change others perspectives and had me read it to the class. I know it had changed my mind, and if she was right, I was glad to share my words with others.

As an adult, I continued to write poetry, tucking those slips of paper away for another time. I also wrote journals, more to hang onto the memories than anything else, but regardless, the writing was a release to me.

One inspiration was accelerated when I became a mother. Watching life through my children's eyes gave me new things from which to write. How they learned helped me write instructional manuals better, making me a better trainer, and later in my career, a better manager.

I continued to write documentation for my company, aiding many employees through the years. Other years I wrote articles for quarterly newsletters for employees. I couldn't get enough opportunities to write; it became a passion.

After I had retired, I began writing a blog, and before I knew it, I had readers telling me how I had inspired them with my words. I was able to help them heal through a loss, or other situations by putting their feelings into words for them. Knowing my writing was something others enjoyed, gained peace from, or generated laughter, brought a new chapter in life—writing a novel.

At the age of 60, I became an Indie author. The day I wrote the last words to my novel, I sat with a feeling of excitement that goes beyond words. Since then, I have published two more books. The second book is a sequel to book one, the third a stand-alone. I continue to blog as subjects, emotions or topics of interest work through my mind. I love writing. I am a strong woman, confident in my ability to give people entertainment through the pages of my books.

The greatest part about retirement is finding you may have other interests for which you become passionate. For me, that was photography. I love it and have become an amateur photographer. I post some of my photography on Facebook and have a website for others to enjoy. So many people tell me how they love my view of life through a camera lens.

Whether writing or capturing a moment in time with a camera lens, there is no greater satisfaction than knowing something you love makes a difference in someone else's life.

I just celebrated my 65th birthday, and looking back, I realize what a survivor I am. I'm proud of who I have become. Retirement is about my children, my grandchildren, my siblings, and my husband. I love traveling, camping, having my family or friends over for dinner, and taking the grandkids to the pool or other outings.

Perhaps I was blessed with a positive attitude; at least according to my grandmother I was...I know I simply believe it is important never to stop trying to make life better.

I am currently working on a fourth novel, which will be book three of my series.

Enjoying the Ride

I keep pushing; I never stop believing in myself. I will always have my words to keep me strong.

Life is a journey, and I'm enjoying the ride.

Mindfulness and Bliss

Written by Dr. Thynn Thynn

Dr. Thynn Thynn/Graton, California: Age 75

I was born and raised in Burma to conservative Theravada Buddhists. When I was twenty-five and a medical intern, I started studying the Abhidhamma (Buddhist psychology and philosophy). It became almost like the great love of my life. Being a young doctor, the hidden parallels with biology and some psychology in the text excited me. I had started to sit in silent meditation at a monastery each Sunday. But in Burma, if you're a woman, you don't go to a monastery by yourself; you have to have a companion, either a woman or a man to accompany you. I stopped going when it was difficult to find a companion to go with me.

I was living in Rangoon and met a writer there who, because of the way I was answering his questions about health and the health care system, encouraged me to write and publish. I liked this engagement and soon jumped the fence from general medicine over to public health. I was a skilled painter as well, and during this time I was invited to participate in an all women's exhibition in Rangoon. It was a historical event.

Then I moved to Bangkok with my husband. We had two babies, and I became a full-time mom; eventually I began to work for the United Nations (U.N.) and the World Health Organization. I also began to teach Buddhism and meditation and write down what we were discussing in the group, which became a book manuscript. Then we moved to the United States, settling in upstate New York and raising two young teenagers.

In 1991, I started visiting California to speak to local groups in Berkeley and San Francisco, and a video of my talk was produced. I started doing an annual teaching circuit, and Spirit Rock Meditation Center invited me. Shortly after that, my book came out: *Living Meditation, Living Insight.*

My students all started asking, "Are you going to start a dharma center?" My son was still in high school, and my daughter was already admitted to Stanford during that year, so it all fell into place. In 1996, we moved to Sebastopol and started a non-profit, religious, Buddhist foundation, and found property in Graton, California. We bought four acres with a century-old ranch house. The center was named Sae Taw

Win II. I began teaching there; I was 59. To be the first woman dhamma teacher to set up her own center in America, and also be the residential teacher was a novelty for the Burmese Theravada tradition.

I started with about 10 American students. When I began building some cedis (traditional Buddhist shrines) in 2001, the Burmese in the Bay Area started to come to the center. Ten years later in 2011, we built 28 shrines within three months, which was an extremely gratifying experience. Young Burmese college students would come and have retreats with me and invite me to give talks at their college. I loved teaching and teacher training: it was my bliss.

I traveled a few times to different centers and places in the U. S., Canada, and Australia to teach. Much was going on at the center besides the teaching retreats; we had ceremonies, festivals, and rituals regularly. In 2009, we started producing classical theatrical plays on the life of the Buddha. Unintentionally, creating these plays grew to be a passion of mine.

I went into semi-retirement in 2013 after almost 15 years living and running the center. Earlier, some students thought that I should write another book, so I've got a manuscript nearly completed. I also returned to my art, doing pen and ink drawings, pastels, watercolors, and oils to while away free time. I was not involved in running the center anymore, but I supervised and kept things going. Getting involved with art is very therapeutic for me; it gives me the portal for my creative juices to run. I find that at this time in my life, this is my true bliss, my true authentic self.

But what is more blissful still is the arrival of my very first grandson. Khine was born in June 2014, and he has changed my whole being, so to say. The child is delightful. He makes me want to live to be 100 years old.

My grandson keeps me going, as does my art and, as always, my devotion to the Theravada Buddhist practice of mindfulness in daily life. After two years of semi-retirement away from the Center, I am picking up the reigns again. I really do not quit!

The Joy of Living

Written by Evelyn Lois Coy

Evelyn Lois Coy

Evelyn Lois Coy/San Diego, California: Age 94

I was born in Chicago, Illinois on August 19, 1921. I lived and worked as a comptometer operator at Sears Roebuck until I joined the Navy Waves in 1942. It was devastating when we were attacked at Pearl Harbor, and I felt that I should do my part, so when I was 21 years old, I joined the Waves. Since there was no boot camp, I was sent directly to Yeoman School in Stillwater, Oklahoma to study administrative and clerical work. When we arrived there, our uniforms were still on the drawing board. I was one of the first enlisted women to be trained for duty.

My first assignment was Washington D.C. Since no barracks were built yet for the Waves, I had to live in a civilian apartment in town and ride the bus to work. Barracks were built across from our offices, which had been a debutante finishing school—it was like a little city of its own with a chapel, florist, and dorms. Incidentally, I

The Joy of Living

was married in this chapel. My mother got into the chapel without ID, and when it was time to leave, the Marines wouldn't let her out; the chaplain had to rescue her!

The offices where I worked had 12-foot electrified fences and Marine guards from Guadalcanal. I had a top-secret classification and was only allowed in the area represented by the color of my badge and my picture ID. I could never tell anyone what work I did in the service. My folks never knew and were scared when they did my FBI check back to my school days. It took 50 years to get in my service jacket that my official title was cryptologist. I worked 8-hour shifts, 6-days a week, working at this time on floor-to-ceiling computers with wheels and toggles.

Washington was an interesting place and had more parades than anywhere else. Roosevelt died in 1945 and what a funeral that was to see. One of the greatest events in my life was when I had tea in the White House with Eleanor Roosevelt. She invited the four branches of service women every week for tea. Eleanor Roosevelt was for women's rights but never received recognition for it. Can you imagine the thrill it was for me, a 21 year old, in the White House, talking to the president's wife? Never in my life would I think something like this could happen to me.

I never regretted my time in the service and

have been very proud to wear the uniform. When I married my husband he was in the Navy. He continued serving for 26 years; he was gone a lot of the time. I raised one son who joined the Air Force and served in Vietnam.

I still work with veterans' organizations. Volunteer work is among the greatest things that one can do. I worked for the City of San Diego Planning Department for 21 years, and after retiring from that job, I mentored in the school system. I am very active in my church and take a water class twice a week. And, I still find time to play golf. I keep in touch with my navy friends and enjoy comradery with them. And yes, at 94 years, I still have not quit, and don't plan to.

Unwilling To Settle

Written by Linda Todd

Linda Todd

Linda Todd/Charleston, Mississippi: Age 67

Many women my age do not want to talk about their age. Age is immaterial to me, and this lady would not go back and try to do anything over. One important reason is that it is useless thinking. Why not prefer to embrace the present and take one day at a time while keeping active, learning something new, and trying to encourage another soul.

Growing up in this little Southern town as a minister's daughter, I was a very quiet youngster with little to say. The youngest of three daughters with a hidden agenda that even I did not know was there.

After finishing high school, my first trip was to Chicago in 1965. My sister and her husband minister pastored there. That did not last too long. I moved back home, and then after a few other stops, marriage was my goal at the young age of twenty.

Unwilling to Settle

Later I started working as an office assistant in this little town in 1977. This job gave me my first experience in processing loan files for rural home loans. It was after seven years that I decided to try out a nursing school in 1984. Proving a point that it could be done at my age, only 34, and I did, with As and Bs.

The only problem was that family survival required more funds than were available, so we decided the best decision was to put family first and get a job. So, that I did.

While not being able to obtain a job within my hometown, we decided again to make a move. This time to Atlanta, Georgia in December of 1985, and it was a very good move for my mortgage-lending career. After only being there less than a week, a position with Freddie Mac gave me another career boost. (Yes, the one that the government took over.) The job while at Freddie was very educational, but as fate would have it, we decided to move closer to home after a couple of years.

We moved to Memphis, Tennessee in 1987, and then I began traveling the states to audit, underwrite, and review mortgage loan files for banks, mortgage companies, and investors. My travel took me from New York to San Francisco, Fort Lauderdale to Seattle, Washington, and a slew of states in between.

Later in 1990, the traveling became too much, and this was when I began my mortgage underwriter career— still learning and gaining more experience to add to my resume. So much more was in store for me. Underwriting is very detailed and learning by the book was best for me. The book is always right, unless, of course, you decide to bend the rules.

With a few additional moves, I became senior vice president of a mortgage broker office. This position ended in 2007 when the mortgage world as we knew it spiraled downward and started the financial crisis that still looms over the country and world.

When having to semi-retire earlier than planned and hating every minute of it, life changed. I wanted to work and of course when you are at a certain age, it is rather hard to explain that you may be a little older, but you have not lost your brain.

With the experience I had gained, my income was far above average for the United States. Working hard was my decision, and being finished was not in my vocabulary.

Having written a Christmas play for church quite a few years before retirement, I had within me the thought that I could write. Writing online began in 2008, along with some contract work. I was still learning and focusing on keeping my mind, body, and soul active. After finishing my first eBook, the plan is to publish it as soon as possible. I will continue with a website (previously four), several blogs, and writing on several article directories. All this keeps me busy, productive, and young. Life begins after so-called "retirement!"

Determination

Written by Rosemary Christie

Determination

Rosemary Christie/Empa, Paphos, Cyprus: Age: 62

I suppose my determination to never give up and never want to quit started at my birth. It came with my first breath, which was labored. Born blue, lacking oxygen, a twin to a boy, I struggled for breath and was incubated, being a premature baby of only seven months duration.

My brother was a sick baby and needed 24-hour attention; so, for the first two years of my life, I survived on very little love, which made me hunger for it all my life. My childhood experiences were confusing, and I had believed you had to suffer to get anything nice. A determination through pain had manifested.

School for me was a haven, which helped me push ahead. Eventually, I was put into a lower class than my brother, and I rose from the bottom of the class to the top. This achievement gave me a resolve to succeed away from comparisons to my twin.

School life was good, and I loved poetry even though I didn't understand what I was reading. I would learn very long poems.

One of my experiences at school was with a senior head teacher, who took us for English and poetry. I was 11 years old. One day she told us that she would give sixpence to the best student for reading. I struggled with reading, as I struggled with most lessons. That beautiful sixpence was never going to be mine, I thought, especially because Mary Jones was brilliant at reading. After we had all read, Mrs. Morgan proclaimed me the winner. She said, "Not because Rosemary read the best, but because she had lots of expression in her reading." My conviction grew even more from then on, and I took her words to mean that I was an achiever. This validation gave me hope, which I took into adulthood.

At the age of 36, I learned transcendental meditation, and this changed my life. For the first time in my life I felt happy. I continued to meditate twice daily; I turned to holistic therapies, like hypnosis and psychotherapy, and became a well sought-after hypnotherapist/psychotherapist, helping people to believe in themselves.

I went on to an eight-month course with Jill Edwards, the author of *Living Magically*, and my work developed along the metaphysical healing

Determination

road. I taught my clients to love themselves and to take responsibility for their lives, knowing that they had created it, and because of that, they could change it. As they changed, so did their partners, friends, and foes. My healing continued; as I taught, I also learned. That need for perfection in me kept me determined to heal.

I became a Science of Mind (SOM) practitioner after studying for ten years over the Internet, and I let go of the past, seeing that it had been a great asset to me. I had grown nearer to God and found out that God wasn't up in heaven but was right inside of me. It was the Living Power that was everything in the universe including me. WOW!

I began to write a book, and a friend helped me edit it, and I self-published it. It went out and has helped many people all over the world. Not a best seller, but a good read because I have had many emails from people telling me how it has helped them. What could be more rewarding than that? I have since written three more books, and never thought that the little child who hated herself so much could achieve this.

My purpose today is to get the message out that we create our reality, and we can change it by changing our thoughts and beliefs. No matter what happens to you; you can win at life just as I have.

Quitting Was Never an Option

Written by Carol Graham

Quitting Was Never an Option

Carol Graham/Bellingham, Washington: Age 67

Only the tapping of metal on wood broke the uncomfortable silence in Randall's Grocery Store. I could feel the tension rise. It was 1953. I was seven. I had gone to the corner store with a group of friends to get our penny candies, which was a regular Saturday afternoon ritual. This particular Saturday would make an impact on me that lasted 50 years.

Mr. Randall reached into the candy bin, picked up the assortment and placed them into the hands of each anxious child. I was barely tall enough to see over the wooden counter, but I stretched above my head and placed my nickel on the top. "A bag please." The big man dug into the bin, picked out the candies, and reached over to place them in my hand. "I would like a bag, please."

Mr. Randall was visibly irritated. I grabbed back the nickel and began tapping it on the counter. With my left hand on my hip, I tapped my right foot in sync. My friends stopped chewing and stared in disbelief. How could anyone so frail, so slight, and so young stand fearlessly before such an enormous man? I had focus and determination. It was as if I knew the first rule of salesmanship: state your position, hold firm, and shut up. No negotiation. No apology. Just silence. Mr. Randall reached under the counter and got a small paper bag, "Thank you," I said smiling as I turned and walked out. He had met his match!

I was born ill but never expected the phone call from the specialist's office asking me to come in as soon as possible. That conversation has been seared into my psyche. It changed my life. The doctor just stared at me, and then glanced around the room. Seconds felt like minutes and then he spoke. There is one word in any language that is difficult to hear. It immediately brings fear, guilt, anger, and an assortment of questions. Why me? How did this happen? It is an ugly word. That word is—cancer. My mother had died of cancer. I was a young woman in my 20s. I was trembling and frightened.

"Carol, basically you have two choices, and I think it is obvious which one you will choose!" I assumed he meant two types of treatment. He continued, "Your choices are hysterectomy or death." He paused for impact. "You are a very sick young woman."

Quitting Was Never an Option

Strength I did not know I had welled up inside of me, and I said, "I do not accept those choices. There has to be another way! I will find that alternative." He replied, "Well then, lady, go home, suffer, and...die!" I stood up and started out of the room, paused, and said, "I will walk in here pregnant!" Within three weeks, I found a new direction–natural medicine. Fourteen years later, I walked into that doctor's office–pregnant!

Shattered dreams, broken promises, and being battered on many fronts my entire life; I knew there would be many people who could relate to my story. Consequently, I published my memoir, *Battered Hope*, but knew nothing about social media, marketing or promoting. Stepping out of my comfort zone at 65, I took every free online course possible learning how to be a success on the Internet. Since publishing, doors are consistently opening for speaking engagements, book tours, interviews, and writing opportunities.

A few months ago, I started my radio show, "Never Ever Give Up Hope," with the unique privilege of interviewing people who have survived insurmountable circumstances and became successful. Their stories are an inspiration and motivation to many who are in turmoil and wondering how they are going to make it. If I had given up at any time in my life, I would not be here now. Both my book and my show were recently discovered, and a prestigious magazine will soon honor me.

I refuse to give up, no matter my age. Inside I am that little girl in the candy store who did not know her life would be so traumatic. But because of that inner strength she had as a child, she never gave up until she got the bag for her candy.

Life is a journey, and I'm enjoying the ride.

Give Up the Bitter Cup

Written By Colette Srebro Hughes

Colette Srebro Hughes/Scott Township, PA: Age 63

She loved to learn. She always did. Others complained about teachers, homework, or tests. Not her. She respected her teachers, did her homework, and never complained about tests. Surely, such admirable qualities would lead that girl to college. But those admirable qualities and intentions were not enough to get her into college when she was eighteen. An abusive and dysfunctional household smothered her love for learning, her scholastic achievement, and her self-confidence. I was that girl.

My father was an alcoholic and a classic male chauvinist. His mantra was, "College degrees are for men only!" As such, my brothers went off to college. Not me. Not then. I was the oldest girl stuck between ten children. My father believed that women should be "barefoot and pregnant." Consequently, I downplayed any scholastic aptitude at home. To survive, I hid my school achievements from my family, but at school I could shine. The classroom was my haven. Each book was my personal escort through far-away places.

My mother also had a faraway place—as far away from my father as she could go. Hoping things would get better after their divorce, we moved to a new city. Despite Mom's good intentions, that new move did not make things any better. Lost in the family milieu and struggling to succeed in the one place that had been my sanctuary, school, I became down-beaten and bitter.

Eventually, I would learn that low self-esteem is often caused by the lack of a nurturing parent. Children of alcoholics experience an excessive sense of responsibility and are overly concerned with the welfare of others. Outwardly, they appear to be smart, articulate, and personable. Inwardly, they try desperately to escape negative thoughts.

I am a child of an alcoholic. Throughout early adulthood, feelings of abandonment, self-pity and an unquenchable need for affection overshadowed many decisions. To excess, I had placed the desires of others ahead of my own. Thus, I did not choose the college degree for which I always longed. I sacrificed my identity as I struggled to make things right for my mother, brothers, and sisters.

At the age of 51, my search for answers to my emotional turmoil had escalated until my inner spirit screamed, "STOP! That's not who I want to be!"

That old cliché is true—"Life can make someone bitter or better." Certainly, I had tasted the bitterness. I discovered that I hated what it was doing to my life. And I hated its heartburn even more. I decided I would not allow bitterness to force-feed my future. It was time to swallow bitterness and seek something better. It was time to pursue my identity.

"College? Who starts college at 51 years old? Am I too old?"

I took a huge first step and enrolled in weekend classes. That was a big challenge because I also had two sons in college during that time. But my old friends, hard work, and determination got me through. I graduated with an Associate Degree: Communications, Summa Cum Laude.

That degree became invaluable to my walk back into wholeness. My life took directions I could only have dreamed about back in my high school days. The cleaning service I established grew to include commercial contracts.

Give Up the Bitter Cup

My success as a female entrepreneur has been featured in local papers along with commendations from Pennsylvania's government officials and the Small Business Development Center at the University of Scranton. It is an honor to serve on the President's Advisory Council at my alma mater, Keystone College. I have served as a mentor to high school and college women and men who are struggling to find their future paths. It is important to admonish them to work for the common good but also to keep learning and striving to maintain their identity.

I'm 63 years old, and I love to learn. I always have. I am that school student of years earlier who loved school, homework, and teachers–the girl who strived to please her family but lost her identity in the process. But I've walked a journey to wholeness, a journey that began when I gave up the bitter cup.

An Awfully Big Adventure

Written by Jude L. Gorgopa

An Awfully Big Adventure

Jude L. Gorgopa/Vancouver, BC: Age 60

I was born in Vancouver, Canada in 1955 and often joke that I held car keys in one hand and a suitcase in the other. Acting, dancing, music appreciation, writing, camping, hiking, and a profound love and respect for animals and nature also came early. I especially adored books. I would often make up my fantastic tales and later on in my teens had a few newspaper articles published, along with winning an award or two from writing contests. When I was 12, I was selected as a volunteer companion for a group of Down syndrome children of assorted ages. This experience influenced me to approach diversity in a very positive way.

In 1976, in my early 20s and out on my own, a whole new world opened up for me. I had learned earlier on that I was not the perfect 9-5 employee, so I explored ways of working on a contract or freelance basis. During that time, I continued my education as an adult student, and I believe that it was a class that I took in communications and public speaking at UBC that pushed me further out.

I then trained as a professional makeup artist for photo, film, and television. I was first signed by an agency based in London and then one from New York. I worked in several areas internationally on both sides of the camera in fashion, TV, and on the stage including as a stylist, fashion editor, and spokesperson. After six years, I moved to New York City. I was just 27 at the time but was told that I was already too old to be a model or start an acting career there.

In 1985, I worked with my future husband-to-be on a photo shoot. He was the photographer, and I was the model. The timing was way off for a relationship so I left NYC for a year in Paris–a last big hurrah before my immigration status had to be upgraded from an H1 visa to a green card. On my return in 1986, I found a company to sponsor me in a corporate position that lasted the five and a half years I had to wait to allow my status to change.

Looking back at my early years in NYC, most of my experiences, particularly in sales, training, and public relations helped me to create new paths toward future opportunities. I felt a breakthrough approaching, and it was time to prepare. At this time, I found a faithful and beautiful companion, a rescue cat named Frankie. He would start my future involvement in an animal rescue group.

In 1991, my future husband re-entered my life. I finally received my green card in early 1993, and we were married the following October. After traveling around Italy together for a month, we returned to our apartment in Manhattan along with Frankie. I quit my job, and my life was in reinvention mode once again. I decided to go back to being self-employed and, among other projects, started coaching actors and other professionals, wrote and taught a curriculum for a private esthetician's school, and worked as a publicist for a singer. I had also begun taking photographs using black and white film, and my husband taught me to use a darkroom to develop my own photos. In 1998, I bought a new apartment for us in the same neighborhood and would eventually set up a home office there.

The year 2,000 was the year I turned 45. I started my current business, Clout Et Cetera, Inc. in April of 2001. I had worked with hundreds of individuals and businesses as a reinvention consultant, small business resource, and mentor helping people with change and several aspects of success. I created a blog and radio show along with writing articles for magazines, was booked for speaking engagements, radio and television interviews, and hosted networking and fundraising events. I have served on boards, earned three coaching and training certifications, and taught my own programs created as an adjunct at NYU, FIT, and Baruch College in NYC. In 2009, British Airways recognized me as a Face of Opportunity. In 2005, I added life, accident, and health insurance to Clout Et Cetera by becoming a licensed insurance agent and later a certified independent broker.

If I were to very briefly sum up my life thus far, I would say that I truly did it my way. There will be many new opportunities and experiences in my 60s and beyond, including a recent foray into politics, more work with Clout Et Cetera, and growing my charitable foundation, Fraidy's Friends. I will also strive to be a positive influence for change and a leader by example for others, particularly my two teenage grandnieces. My awfully big adventure continues...and I simply refuse to quit!

Going on When Others Quit

Written by LaVonne Mahugh

LaVonne Mahugh

LaVonne Mahugh/Des Moines, Washington: Age 84

I was born in rural North Dakota in 1931 to a very poor farm family struggling through the Great Depression. My mother had a nervous breakdown when I was about six years old and spent a long period as an invalid, so in addition to the material poverty there was also a degree of emotional poverty. But somehow, in spite of this early life, my three brothers and I all graduated from college and became contributing members of society.

An unexpected event happened to me just before my 59th birthday. I came home from work to find my husband, Dick, on the floor–paralyzed on his entire left side from a massive stroke. I had no say in the matter, and I felt like a victim of circumstances beyond my control.

When my husband had a stroke, I was living a typical American life. I was the mother of four grown sons, a registered nurse with a part time job married to a chemical engineer, and living in suburban Seattle. I was satisfied with my life. I had always dreamed of traveling, but I knew I would be caring for him, at this point. For six months, I gave it my best. When he was hospitalized in July 1991, I told the social worker that he could not be discharged home to my care, so he was discharged to a nursing home instead. This decision to divorce was foreign to my basic value system. Once I made that decision, I had a terrible time accepting myself for doing it. I looked back over my life to see what had helped me most through difficult times.

One event that I felt had been helpful was a series of personal growth seminars that I had taken a few years before. It had forced me to get out of my comfort zone in my thinking on several levels. This program had a free audit privilege, so I could re-take it for free. It was at a support group meeting during the third level of this course when something happened, that I felt jarred me out of my rut and ended up changing the course of my life.

Our monthly meetings allowed for each of us to have 30 minutes to share what was going on in our life. Then we could ask the group to either help us figure out what to do or support us in what we decided to do.

After several months of meeting with this group, this young man in the group said to me, "LaVonne, if all you are going to do is whine about the sad state of affairs since your husband's stroke, I am just going to tune you out. I am not going to listen to that anymore. I am sorry that your husband had a stroke, but there is nothing I can do to change that. Unless you can come up with something positive to do with your life, I don't know how to support you. And I will no longer be a party to just sympathizing with you as you wallow in your despair."

I remember hearing about a citizen diplomacy trip to India, Nepal, and Tibet. I went on that trip, and it changed my life. When we landed in Madras, India, the first thing we saw on the TV was the U.S. State Department issuing a warning to American citizens not to go to India. There was internal unrest in that country, and many airports were being bombed. We decided to continue with our plans. If we had returned home in fear, I would never have had the amazing opportunities I had. I shook hands with Mother Teresa, and I drove across the high Himalayan Mountains on what was then a dirt and gravel road.

There were no restrooms or other facilities on this road then (1993), so we would just try and find some privacy behind an outcropping of rock to relieve ourselves. As I was sitting on this rock and surveying that Tibetan Plateau, I thought, "Here I am, on the opposite side of the planet and at the top of the world."

To date, I have visited over 28 countries, on five continents, with various groups, family members and grandchildren over the years. I have felt more alive than ever. So by refusing to quit, I have learned much and plan to continue to have adventures for life.

Can't Stop-Won't Stop

Written By Sharon Boone

Can't Stop Won't Stop

Sharon Boone/Centreville, Virginia: Age: 60

More than *anything*, she LOVED to look through the fashion and beauty pages of Ebony, Jet, and Essence magazines, gazing at beautiful faces with brown skin that matched her own. The teenager's quest to duplicate the perfection displayed on those colorful magazine layouts ranged from bleaching her skin to trying every cosmetic and hair product, and even accidentally shaving off her eyebrows. This fascination also led her down some not-so-beautiful paths, like sleeping in a friend's car, as she pressed toward her passion. **Can't stop–won't stop.**

My name is Sharon Boone, and I was that young woman. I could have quit many times but today I'm the president of Flori Roberts, Inc., a popular cosmetic brand designed for women of color and the first black cosmetics sold in upscale department stores. I'm also the president of Color Me Beautiful Inc., the world leader in women's color analysis!

First, I must thank God for these 60+ years of life. Through Him, I've experienced a deep love, hope, and guiding light. "For I know the thoughts that I think toward you, says the LORD, thoughts of peace and not of evil, to give you a future and a hope." (Jeremiah 29:11 – NKJV) Walk with me for just a few minutes, while I remember.

Father was a musician and teacher, and Mother–trained in business–worked in medical records and ran our household. I began piano lessons at age 5 (and still love to play today for personal enjoyment) but increasingly focused my career dreams toward the fashion and beauty industry, as I grew older. When high school graduation loomed, I made it unequivocally clear that I planned to study fashion. My parents made it unequivocally clear that I would NOT: their financial support would only extend to academic/collegiate studies –not to fashion school.

Off to college I went, studying music because it seemed a fitting progression from what I'd been doing, but two years later, with mounting frustration, I could no longer do it. Announcing my decision to drop out of school, my parents' loving response was, "That's fine, but you'll need to get a job, Sharon."

Hmmm...work...school...work...suddenly school didn't seem so bad. I returned, changing my major to psychology with a minor in sacred music. I worked part-time selling Flori Roberts cosmetics, an experience that fueled my exuberance for beauty and fashion. I couldn't wait to leave home after graduation to pursue my dreams!

First stop: Spokane, Washington—where my brother lived; hated it. Next stop: Atlanta, Georgia—no home or job. A family friend let me stay in a damp garage that smelled like dogs, so I opted to sleep in a friend's car in her driveway. Desperate, and remembering my cosmetics experience, I called and asked to speak to Flori Roberts, herself! **Can't stop—won't stop.**

They put me through to her: I'm not sure who was more shocked and surprised—Ms. Roberts or me. Quickly composing and introducing myself, I boldly told her I wanted to work in her public relations department. Flori Roberts was intrigued by my tenacity and facilitated the employment that kick-started my God-ordained journey.

I began selling Flori Roberts cosmetics at what is now Macy's Department stores, and soon became a makeup artist. I was subsequently promoted to account manager, then regional sales manager. When Ivax Corporation acquired Flori Roberts in 1994, I was sent to Chicago as the national sales manager, now with a 7-year-old daughter in tow. Several months later, I was promoted to vice president of sales, then to vice president of sales and marketing. Ivax allowed me to spread my wings in this latest role, bringing renowned singer Patti LaBelle on board as a spokesperson and acquiring the Iman cosmetics line. Ultimately, I became the President of Flori Roberts Inc. **Can't stop—won't stop.**

My heart bursts with gratitude as I thank God for each new day and opportunity. He helped me flow with the twists and turns of my journey and through His strength, I never quit. I encouraged my daughter to seek and chase her passion, just as I did. Today, she is doing exactly that, performing on Broadway. My exuberance for the beauty business is as vibrant and strong as ever, but God's love has revealed how my business can expand to transform women's lives. My daily fuel is provided through prayer and reading God's Word. Enjoying life despite the challenges, I've learned to trust an unknown future to an all-knowing God who leads me. Whatever is to come, quitting is not an option!

Be Empowered

Written by Colette Michelle

Colette Michelle

Colette Michelle/San Diego, California: Age 85

I was born in Angoulême, France about a decade before World War II. We lived under the German occupation and suffered through hard food rationing. I remember writing "Vive De Gaulle" on the walls behind the backs of the German soldiers. I assisted my mother in helping the Jews escape from northern France into Free France. My father was a captured prisoner in Calais and sent to Oflag 4D in Dresden, Germany for the rest of the war.

My mother was very domineering, which left me with a strong desire to be "center stage" at a very early age. I wanted to be an actress, something not done at that time in a French family. After the war, I was sent to a finishing school in England; then to the University of Madrid, Spain, where I met my first husband, married, and had two daughters.

Be Empowered

Upon moving to San Diego, CA, I discovered my dreams could be achieved, as America was the land of more freedom and opportunities. The first thing I did was to learn how to drive. With a penchant and an eye for fashion, I began "image consulting" (when the profession was in its infancy) to help both women and men learn how to look their very best. San Diego and Los Angeles were both far from being fashion heaven. Being born French and having a French accent helped me tremendously in this fashion business. I used it to my advantage. I decided to form my first company "Fashion Promotions Unlimited."

I began by doing informal modeling in restaurants even though I was a "petite," under 5'3," which at that time was not a model size. Luck struck again when someone told me I had a gift for speaking. Before long, people dubbed me the "Dr. Ruth of Image." My presentations were straight forward, no-nonsense, humorous, and informative.

My next goal was to break into the corporate market, so I changed my company's name to "Winning Images International." Through my persistence and hard work more opportunities came my way—conventions booked me for "spouse" programs. At last money was coming in. Large corporations and financial institutions around the United States, such as Avis and Coca-Cola, were calling me. They flew me in, dined me, and paid well. I was in heaven! All this gave me more courage and persistence to prevail in creating new ideas. I was the first image consultant to present accessory shows for the international and USA buyer at the Los Angeles Mart.

The best came when I was chosen the corporate fashion director of the 13 Walker Scott Stores based in San Diego. The CEO of the company sent me to the London and Paris fashion weeks. WOW! That I was asked to present fashion shows enabled me to use "Broadway-style" singing and dancing for the event, and diverse types of models, even animals on the catwalk.

I left Walker Scott Co. to visit my second husband who was in the Pacific during the Vietnam War. I spent four months traveling by myself around the world on Pan Am. It was a daring thing to do at that time. Beginning in San Diego heading west, I flew Pan Am to Hong Kong and Singapore and even visited Nepal, which just opened its borders. Then India, and the brand new country, Israel, Italy, the Netherlands, and finally back to the States. No need to tell you that being blond, petite, and sexy equated to lots of free dinner offers. The trip enabled me to gather colorful material as well as great stories along the way.

Be Empowered

Over the years, working with clients has allowed me to empower them to find their confidence and strength. This is what has kept me going. Now in the autumn of my life at 85, having triumphed over cancer, I continue to teach fashion and beauty classes for a national organization catering to adults over 60.

I am having a ball. Life is a kick, and I know that I still can learn and accomplish challenges no matter what my age while I have the desire and passion that is still in me. What I did most of my life was to take stock of liabilities, turn them into assets, and accentuate the assets I had.

The important word is never, ever quit!

Forever the Teacher

Written By Merle R. Saferstein

Forever the Teacher

Merle R. Saferstein/North Miami Beach, FL:
Age 70

My mother, a teacher for over fifty years, clearly influenced my decision to enter the field of education. During my long and wonderful career as an educator, I taught in an elementary school and a pre-school, worked as an administrative assistant in a high school, and directed both a pre-school and a day camp with 350 campers and a staff of seventy-five counselors.

In the early '80s, I quit working in education and began writing. I spent over two years walking along the ocean, filling countless journals, and completing a novel.

In 1985, I had the opportunity to bring the photographic exhibition *Anne Frank in the World: 1929 – 1945* to Miami. In the six weeks that the exhibition was in South Florida, more than 60,000 people viewed it. I lectured to over one hundred groups of students and adults, sharing the story of Anne Frank, the Holocaust, and the dangers of prejudice.

That experience led me to become the director of educational outreach at the Holocaust Documentation and Education Center in South Florida. My job was to plan and implement our speakers' bureau, which addressed over 18,000 students a year, the teachers' training institutes, an annual national writing and visual arts contest, and the Student Awareness Days that served as prejudice reduction programs for those in high school and college. We touched the lives of tens of thousands of students and teachers each year. I had the privilege of working closely with over four hundred Holocaust survivors, ensuring that the younger generations learned from their legacies.

As I approached my mid-sixties, after twenty-six years at the Holocaust center, I decided to retire at age 67. I had fulfilled my mission and was ready to move on. Knowing that I still wanted to write, speak, teach, and volunteer, I walked out the door with a plan for the future.

Upon retirement, I immediately set out to write *Room 732*, a book of short stories, which I completed and published within a year. That was the beginning of making my dream come true for the next part of my life.

Forever the Teacher

As a result of my work with Holocaust survivors, I understood the important role legacy plays in one's life. I developed a class called Living and Leaving Your Legacy^{SM} and have since taught over twenty eight-week classes helping people understand that how they live their lives is their legacy. I also facilitate workshops and speak on the subject both locally and nationally.

I currently volunteer with a hospice organization visiting patients, train various hospice staffs on legacy work, plan and participate in a bereavement camp for children who have lost family members, and help dying individuals do some form of sacred legacy work to leave for their loved ones. Also as a volunteer, I teach a bi-monthly writing class at Gilda's Club, a resource and support center for women who have or had cancer.

Last summer when I toured India, I visited a slum school. Since then, I have paired the students at that school with those at a day school in Miami. The children and teachers in both schools now exchange letters and are learning about one another's cultures. Also, the Miami students raised $1,200 and purchased backpacks and much-needed school supplies for the children in India.

What is most exciting to me at age 70 is that my life is filled with meaningful endeavors. My schedule is fuller than it has ever been as I continue to lead a vibrant life.

One of the things I have appreciated ever since turning 60 has been the wisdom that has come from all my years of living. With the passage of time, my perspective has changed as I view experiences through a broader lens. I understand now what matters most. I am happiest when connecting with others and experiencing the love that comes with my relationships. Above all, I realize that how I live my life is the legacy I will leave behind.

On the Way to 105

Written by Mary McCormack

Mary McCormack/Jacksonville, FL: Age 62

As the youngest child, I was spunky and chatty. My father was an officer in the Army Counter-Intelligence Corps. At age six, I remember putting my hands on my hips declaring, "Daddy, you need to listen to me because I have something important to say!" Amused, he looked down and said, "What is so important?" In my young mind, everything was important and my voice needed to be heard. It was probably the beginning of my career as a professional speaker.

At age eleven, my life changed drastically when we moved from Virginia to Oberammergau, Germany. Life was so different living in the Alps. On a school trip, we gathered chestnuts to provide winter food for the reindeer in the forest! After six months, we relocated to Verona and Vicenza, Italy. I enjoyed the languages, experiences and friends.

Two years later in Fayetteville, North Carolina, things were different because we were different. Travel and living overseas gives you a unique perspective on the world and other cultures. I discovered that I loved languages and studied French, Italian, German, Spanish and Latin. As a high school senior, I planned a post-graduation summer trip and worked part-time as a school bus driver to finance the trip. I traveled alone and explored Iceland, Brussels, Austria, France, Germany, Switzerland and Italy. Experiences can create a domino effect in your life. Becoming fluent in French earned me extra college credits and I graduated with a psychology degree in three years. I worked and also served as captain of the college women's varsity fencing team. Within a three week period, I turned 21, graduated from college and got married.

Your life can travel on the straight path that you plan for until something totally unexpected happens. My life was forced to take a sharp turn in another direction when as a new mother of my six month old son, my dermatologist grimly told me, "Mary, this mole is melanoma cancer. You need to see a surgeon today." The thought of not watching my son grow up was chilling. I gave myself two weeks to cry about the injustice of having cancer at age 27. Then I realized how much time and energy I was expending on something I had no control over. What if I live to be 105 instead of dying within a year as most patients diagnosed at that time did? I decided not to waste a second of the life I had with my family and friends.

The surgery caught the cancer in time, and clearly it was not my time to leave. I had a second son six years later. I worked as a healthcare volunteer services administrator and developed a professional speaking business specializing in training at state, national and international conferences. I loved my work and my life.

After fifteen years of marriage, my life changed direction again with an amicable divorce. Two years later, I married my forever husband. In this marriage deal, I got a husband whom I enjoy more every day, two special stepsons (and later their dear wives and caring children), an Australian mother-in-law who became my second mother and a fluffy dog named Justin. It was a very, good deal! At age 62 on the way to 105, my faith, family, friends, and work give me tremendous joy. I have survived 25 surgeries including cancer, and yet, I have never had anything that could not be endured with a positive attitude, strong faith, skilled physicians and supportive family and friends. My life journey continues to have unexpected twists and turns, some challenging and some joyful. My newest granddaughter makes me laugh when she tries to kiss me when we visit via my iPad. I am grateful for every day that I grow older, wiser and more seasoned in new life experiences. It is still a long way to 105!

MY STORY

Joyce Knudsen, Ph.D.

Joyce Knudsen, Ph.D.

Joyce Knudsen, Ph.D./Nashville, Tennessee: Age 71

I can still remember having "guts" as a child. If someone said something to me, I would always respond, "What did you say?" I needed clarification so I would not take words the wrong way. Growing up in school, I worked hard to maintain grades, given that I was like a mother to my sisters and brothers and responsible for them throughout childhood. The responsibility didn't make me weaker—it made me stronger.

When it came time to go to college, the finances were not there, so I worked and put away money in order to get an education. One year working and one year going to school was the only way it could happen. It took eight years, but I refused to do it any other way.

To earn money for college, I worked as an automobile title clerk for a used car dealer. It was a humbling experience meeting so many people and learning about their lifestyles. From this, I

My Story

grew, as I had from all my previous experiences. When the time was right, I decided to take what I had gleaned from my experiences and try my hand as a consultant.

It was at this time that I married and had two children. I learned to give and take from them, which enriched my life. At the time, I was living in Detroit, and my first job was at a finishing school. It was at this time I started working on my college degrees and earned a Ph.D. at the age of 52.

It was time for me to begin a consulting business. My first client was a woman of wealth who had been in a coma for six months. Prior to that, she was a well-known, successful member of the community. My job was to help her to walk, talk, and learn all that she had forgotten while in the coma. Assisting her was yet another humbling experience. The result: she returned to normalcy and opened her own business and is now a successful business person in Detroit. Her parents felt they owed me, but I felt I owed them for giving me the experience of working with such a lovely person, willing and wanting to re-learn.

Another wonderful experience was when a female client yearned to become the first president of the American Veterinarian Association. We worked on every aspect of both verbal and nonverbal communication. We focused on her appearance, behavior, and communication. Following is a testimonial from LinkedIn that, once again, humbled me.

Dr. Joyce Knudsen assisted me during a time of great transition: from private veterinary practitioner to campaigning for a national office. She was realistic, highly skilled in her understanding of the challenges we were facing in this environment, and exceptionally effective in the recommendations she made. Joyce was one of the people who made my success possible.

After these two experiences, I knew my life's work would be consulting. I learned that a person could start something he/she had never done before and make it work.

Since that time, I have worked in the Image Management Field and reached my way to the top of this industry, becoming the first AICI CIM (Certified Image Master). Few have attained this award. Knowing that diversification is important, I embarked upon writing books, tutoring authors, and mastering social media. On Twitter, I have met many contacts and now have one million followers. On Google Plus, I worked hard to reach 20,000+ people and have had wonderful Google chats over the years. On Facebook, people who

My Story

were once unknown to me have become great friends.

Lastly, on LinkedIn, with 8,000+ connections, I can go directly to ask for valuable advice and direction. Social sites, for me, turned out to be another humbling experience.

I have no intentions to stop having these wonderful experiences. I am a woman who refuses to quit, no matter the circumstances or what comes along. I can't wait to explore options that will help me further enrich and grow throughout the rest of my life.

5

The Virtues of Aging

Who decides when we are old? We do! Each of us becomes old when we think we are old. We age more quickly when we have counterproductive attitudes. A life of dormancy and dependence on others invites a substantial limitation on our physical and mental activity, as would making the choice to restrict the number of people with whom we interact. People who face the aging process with anguish, fear, and unnecessary stress fall victim to the perils of old age.

We can look at the aging process positively by realizing that we are in our latter years, and we can choose to do so with goals and dreams, and certainly with great happiness. This more positive mindset is NOT selfish, as it will open up stronger relationships with others.

Refusing to Quit

Sociologists have written numerous studies about the major predictors of successful aging.

They are:

- The amount of education we have attained
- The degree of physical activity we have maintained
- The degree of control we feel we have over our destiny

An elaborate study at The McArthur Foundation concluded that the three elements of successful aging are as follows:

- Avoiding disease and disability
- Maintaining mental and physical function
- Continuing engagement in life

The latter involves keeping up our relationships with others and performing productive activities. This "engagement in living" requires adapting; making successful adjustments to the changing conditions we have to face, which will inevitably involve responsibilities, challenges, difficulties, and pain. These experiences will keep us closer to others, hence allowing us to develop more self-respect and mastery over our lives which is very critical to a life of peace and tranquility.

Sigmund Freud summed it up perfectly when he said,

"The essentials of human life are work and love."

Some of the greatest gifts we can give ourselves as older adults are to stay active, healthy, and expect change. Additionally, helping others adds to the quality of our lives.

Seniors are valuable in society as they finally have the time to help the disadvantaged or physically-challenged and involve themselves in community efforts; they are a saving grace to many.

So, what is good about getting old? In researching and preparing to write this book, I have learned a simple truth. Some people like getting old while others do not. In a social site poll, there were many reasons why people liked getting old. Some are:

- I can do what I want.
- I have a lot of gratitude for becoming old when others have not.
- I have my weekends back.
- My kids are grown up.
- I have more time to travel.
- I have a chance to pursue my dreams.

- I have more time to volunteer.
- I can give back to the community now.
- I don't need to have a professional wardrobe anymore.
- I can search for love.
- I don't have to look attractive all the time.
- I get to spend more time with the people I care about.
- Some said, "This is the happiest time in my life."

6

Summary and Conclusions:

It has been an eye-opening experience to write this book. Women came forward with amazing stories of why they refuse to quit.

Perhaps the older we get, the more likely we are to have developed our mind-sets and habits, locking us into fixed ways of thinking and working. There is now, however, increasingly a challenge to this preconception that many of us find rings so true.

Professor William R. Klemm at Texas University suggests that for people who stay healthy and mentally active, brain function need not decline with age. Klemm goes on to say, "Too many seniors resign themselves to the ravages of age. They will find, however, large benefits from challenging themselves in new experiences and competencies. Better yet, learning new things makes you feel good about yourself, especially when accomplishing things other people think you can't do."

Moreover, there is an increasing body of evidence showing that when people continue to learn, their brain shows signs of plasticity, which will help prevent age-related decline in brain activity. Creativity requires experience, knowledge and original thinking. It is no surprise, therefore, that many of the artists like Picasso, Cezanne, and Verdi came into their own in later years.

This challenge to age and stereotyping is as relevant in the business world as it is in the creative domain. A recent report on talent in the workplace by PwC reported that of the 6,000 European professionals surveyed, the largest proportion of strategist leaders were found to be female and over the age of 55. "This is an area of talent often overlooked," said Jessica Leitch, people and organization consultant at PwC. The strategist leader takes the long view, has big-picture thinking and can handle complexity—just what is needed in the somewhat turbulent times we live in where change is constant. There is a strong argument for encouraging and enabling women to stay in the workforce as they age instead of overlooking them.

One commentary on this report comes from, Age at Work director at Business in the Community, Rachael Saunders. She blames this on an unconscious bias in the workplace and advocates for specialist training to eradicate this bias. "Nobody intends to discriminate," she says, "but we all have these biases that say women of a certain age don't make good managers or that it's time for them to retire." Google has been running workshops lately to challenge unconscious bias in their workplace.

Eradicating the "ageism" bias from the workplace goes beyond basic fairness. Companies are more successful when their employees feel young for their age. A study of over 15,000 employees from 107 companies found that workers who felt much younger than their chronological age more often met goals they had promised their managers. The enhanced performance by these thriving individuals made for companies with higher financial gains, more efficient outcomes, and a longer tenured workforce. An employee's "young at heart" attitude was fostered by organizations with age-inclusive policies and an atmosphere where "employees felt their work was more important and meaningful."

As Dr. Marla Gottschalk, an industrial and organizational psychologist says: *"Ultimately, it is not age that matters; it is how we adapt to the changing nature of the workplace, manage to still love what we do and contribute. This is likely true throughout our career lives."*

According to AARP, in 2011 the first of the baby boomers reached what used to be known as retirement age. For the next 18 years, boomers will be turning 65 at the rate of 8,000 per day. The rapid aging of our societies and how much longer the years in retirement are has become an international phenomenon.

Whether we continue in a career path or retire in the traditional sense, we have a variety of capabilities–the goal lies in actively aging. Fortunately, we are being redefined as more and more mediums, such as advertising and television, are representing baby boomers and beyond as vital, creative, sexual, and socially active individuals.

In the end, it is what photographer, Anthony Epes, noted about creativity: "It's not just about giving yourself something to do when you retire or as a replacement for your job, it's about weaving into your life a sense of exploration, a way to enhance your life every day. It doesn't matter what age you come to it (15, 45, 85) because at each point in life you have something to reveal, something to explore."

Joyce Knudsen, Ph.D.

Epilogue:

As Dr. Shefali suggests, and these stories highlight, being true to who we are, at our deepest core, is the ultimate aim. It is the wellspring of strong women everywhere and especially for women in the "forgotten generation." In the end, authenticity, attitude, and action will carry the day–and adapting will be our just reward.

Dr. Joyce exemplifies this noble path. In the midst of incredible visual challenges, she wrote this book and lived the motto "pay it forward" by giving others the chance to tell their story. She demonstrates the ideal of loving work and life, having goals, pursuing them, and being productive and generous–inspiring us to choose reasons to "refuse to quit."

Every essay between these covers sparks a desire to live the adage. Such storytelling offers a vantage point that invites emulation. The vicarious journey is a discovery, time and again, that our response to life's demands determines destiny. Accepting what cannot change is crucial, but changing what can be changed is imperative. We witness how perseverance, confidence, self-efficacy, and believing in our gifts emerge and energize.

These stories motivate us to get on the balance beam and challenge our every step, engage in groups, and continue efforts towards self-actualization. When we, literally, challenge our sense of balance, we move towards thriving as we age. Studies have shown that doing so increases working memory by 50 percent. Be encouraged by super-centenarian, Jeane Calment (who has the longest confirmed human lifespan); at 100 years of age she learned how to ride a bicycle. Our posture, too, influences our mind; stand in a power pose like a superwoman for two minutes and you will become more confident.

Envisioning the person we want to become in the future also helps to motivate us. This is said to be a psychologically difficult skill, but highly effective. We most often project into the future to pursue goals or regulate emotions. As we anticipate various outcomes, their consequences, and a necessary plan of action, we increase our flexible and adaptable nature. We then more readily reach our desired outcome.

Likewise, deep reflection reaching back into childhood and our earliest relationships, and ever-maturing experiences, informs our sense of self and what we value. Such examination is a requirement for a fuller understanding of ourselves; for it is this thorough knowing that allows us to answer questions vital to living a life of meaning, and projecting our authentic course moving forward.

No matter how we remember the past, it's beneficial to begin from a more positive point of view. The lifting of any blame or shame unburdens anxiety and allows us to accentuate our strengths and acknowledge supportive social relationships. From this more positive foundation of our life story newfound possibilities flourish.

Achieving a satisfactory or, better yet, outstanding life is always with us. For as long as we live, our personal history never really comes to an end. We are constantly changing. As positive psychologist, Dan Gilbert, argues: *"Time is a powerful force, it transforms our preferences, it shapes our values, and it alters our personality."*

It's exciting to remember our past and consider the future. Telling stories is a universal phenomenon of ancient origins—it is the heart of our humanity. We, as well as cultures and societies, are not static or homogenous, nor reducible to essential qualities. An event is not an experience sufficient unto itself; it occurs at a specific time and place. In the end, there is no clear picture of a particular person, event, or culture. There is a story of the participant(s) that demonstrates the hybrid quality of self and culture.

The late philosopher, Richard Rorty, claimed that it is through sentimental stories that we can develop the necessary virtue of sympathy. In this way, we have "an increasing ability to see the similarities between ourselves and people very unlike us as outweighing the differences." This concept rests upon our species' unique capacity for education as well as the flexible nature of our mind and character. It gives hope to humanity that the collective mind will foster ever more peace. As the late literary critic and ethicist Wayne Booth said, "The most important of all critical tasks is to participate in–and thus to reinforce–a critical culture, a vigorous conversation, that will nourish in return those who feed us with their narratives."

Joyce Knudsen, Ph.D.

Long Life

By Elaine Feinstein

Late Summer. Sunshine. The eucalyptus tree.
It is a fortune beyond any deserving
to be still *here*, with no more than everyday worries,
placidly arranging lines of poetry.
I consider a stick of cinnamon
bound in raffia, finches
in the grass, and a stubby bush
which this year mothered a lemon.
These days I speak less of death
than the mysteries of survival. I am
no longer lonely, not yet frail, and
after surgery, recognise each breath
as a miracle. My generation may not be
nimble but, forgive us,
we'd like to hold on, stubbornly
content – even while ageing.

REFERENCES:

Aging With Attitude: Growing Older With Dignity and Vitality by Robert Levene, M.D. 2004-2008 PRAEGER: Westport, CT, London

The Virtues of Aging by Jimmy Carter, Random House: Ballantine Publishing Group: 1998

Aging Our Way: Lessons for Living from 85 and Older by Meika Loe: Oxford University Press; 2011

Successful Aging by John W. Rowe, M.D. and Robert L. Kahn, Ph.D. Random House: 1998

Rules for Aging: A Wry and Witty Guide to Life by Roger Rosenblatt: Harcourt, Inc., San Diego, NY, London 2000

Aging Well: The Surprising Guideposts to a Happier Life from the landmark Harvard Study of Adult Development by George E. Vaillant, M.D. Little Brown and Company 2002

Joyce Knudsen, Ph.D.

Naomi's Guide to Aging Gracefully: Facts, Myths, and Good News for Boomers: Simon and Schuster 2007

Aging as a Spiritual Practice: A Contemplative Guide to Growing Older and Wiser by Lewis Richmond Gotham Books: Published by The Penguin Group 2012

Sixty Things to Do When You Turn Sixty Edited by Ronnie Sellers Productions 2006

Shock of Gray: The Aging of the World's Population and How it Pits Young Against Old, Child Against Parent, Worker Against Boss, Company Against Rival and Nation Against Nation by Ted C. Fishman. Scribner: A division of Simon and Schuster, Inc. 2010

Department of Labor, Bureau of Labor Statistics (BLS); U.S. Census Bureau; AARP; Sloan Center on Aging and Work

Kunze, F., Raes, A., and Bruch, H. (2015). It Matters How Old You Feel: Antecedents and Performance Consequences of Average Relative Subjective Age in Organizations. *Journal of Applied Psychology* DOI: 10.1037/a0038909

Istance, D. (2015), Learning in Retirement and Old Age: an agenda for the 21st century. European Journal of Education, 50: 225–238. doi:10.1111/ejed.12120

"Self-Esteem Development From Young Adulthood to Old Age: A Cohort-Sequential Longitudinal Study," Ulrich Orth, PhD, University of Basel, Kali H. Trzesniewski, PhD, University of Western Ontario and Richard W. Robins, PhD, University of California, Davis; *Journal of Personality and Social Psychology*, Vol. 98, No. 4.

ABOUT THE AUTHOR

Dr. Joyce Knudsen received her Bachelors of Arts in Communication and a Masters of Arts in Business Administration, a comprehensive management training program recognized worldwide. Joyce has earned a Ph.D. in Human Services, with an emphasis on self-image and psychology.

Refusing to Quit

Joyce takes pride in what she does. Her keen sense of business, strong educational background and support of her husband led her to the development of The ImageMaker, Inc.®in 1985. This company continues to specialize in helping people to understand the importance of a strong and positive self-image.

For two years Joyce produced and hosted a daily television program, geared toward professional image enhancement and self-esteem. She has been featured in local and national newspapers, and has appeared on several local radio and television talk shows. Joyce now has her own radio show, streamlined worldwide at www.imagemakerincmedia.com

Joyce is a pioneer in her field having developed the first and only International Elite and Coaching Certification Program in the world awarding 8 CEU credits by AICI (The Association of Image Consultants, International). She has the coveted distinction of receiving the first CIM (Certified Image Master), the highest achievement in the Image Industry, through AICI. In addition, Joyce was recognized at a banquet by her peers with the 2001 IMMIE AWARD (Image Makers Merit of Industry Excellence) for her work in the Image Industry.

Some of her interviews include USA Today, Glamour Magazine, New York Times Magazine,

Indianapolis Star, Detroit News and Free Press and The Tennessean newspaper, Women's World and The Chinese Morning Press.

Dr. Joyce specializes in radio celebrity interviews, is an author of over 10 books and works with Image & coaching students, worldwide.

Joyce owes her achievements to a fundamental understanding of, not only herself, but others as well. Indeed, Joyce has learned what it takes to be successful – both in private and professional life.

By working with individuals, organizations and companies in many different industries, Dr. Joyce Knudsen is sharing her powerful insights into human nature. She is helping people to bring out their best in everything that they do. Joyce knows that happiness must precede success – that inner strength that we all carry within ourselves. She also knows that success is within reach of anyone.

You can listen to Dr. Joyce's radio broadcasts at http://www.youtube.com/user/TheImageMakerInc

You can reach Dr. Joyce through her website at www.drjoyceknudsen.com

Connect with Joyce:

Facebook - http://on.fb.me/1JIvfEL
http://on.fb.me/1KRoMwi   &
http://on.fb.me/1fc6ia7
Instagram: http://bit.ly/1EGJlsy
Pinterest: http://bit.ly/1zaRbZ5
LinkedIn: http://linkd.in/1EGJBHP
Twitter: https://twitter.com/following
Google + link: http://bit.ly/1DA3N8z
Amazon Page: http://amzn.to/1OVMAM2
RebelMouse: http://drjoyceknudsen.com/my-social-stream/

Joyce Knudsen, Ph.D.

Other Titles
by Dr. Joyce Knudsen

From Head to Soul for Men, Daily Guide to Personal Style and Inner Self Confidence

From Head to Soul for Women, Daily Guide to Personal Style and Inner Self Confidence

From Head to Soul International

Successful Failures: Wisdom to Inspire You

The Generational Puzzle

Symbols: The Art of Communication

And more!

Made in the USA
San Bernardino, CA
17 October 2016